LUDOVICO EINAUDI

In a Time Lapse

CHESTER MUSIC
part of The Music Sales Group
London/New York/Paris/Sydney/Copenhagen/Berlin/Madrid/Hong Kong/Tokyo

Published by
Chester Music
14-15 Berners Street, London W1T 3LJ, UK.

Exclusive Distributors:
Music Sales Limited
Distribution Centre, Newmarket Road,
Bury St Edmunds, Suffolk IP33 3YB, UK.
Music Sales Pty Limited
Units 3-4, 17 Willfox Street, Condell Park, NSW 2200, Australia.

Order No. CH80982
ISBN: 978-1-78305-006-2
This book © Copyright 2013 Chester Music.

Arranged for solo piano by the composer.
Additional arrangements by Derek Jones.
Edited by Jenni Norey.
Music Processed by Paul Ewers Music Design.
Printed in the EU.

Corale

Music by Ludovico Einaudi

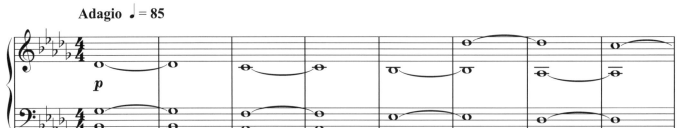

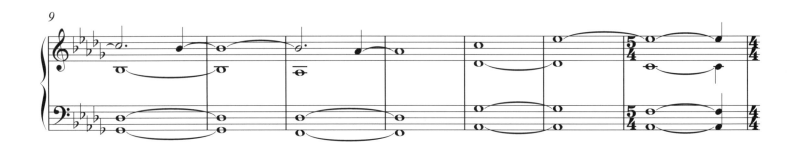

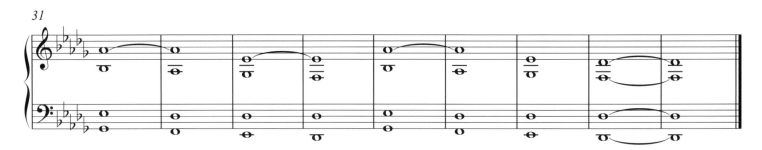

Time Lapse

Music by Ludovico Einaudi

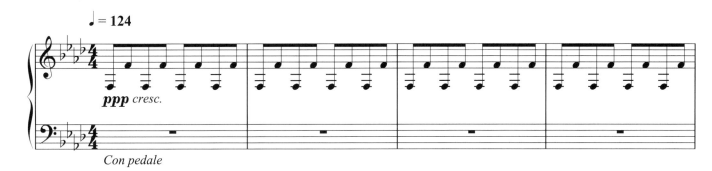

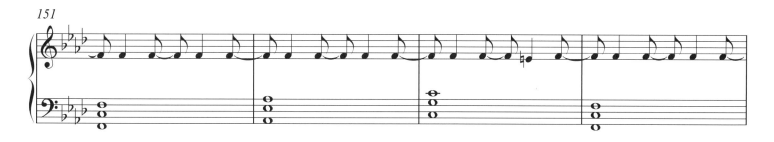

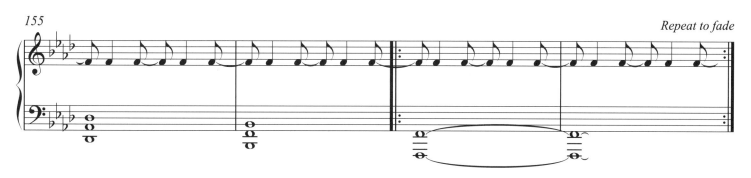

Life

Music by Ludovico Einaudi

15

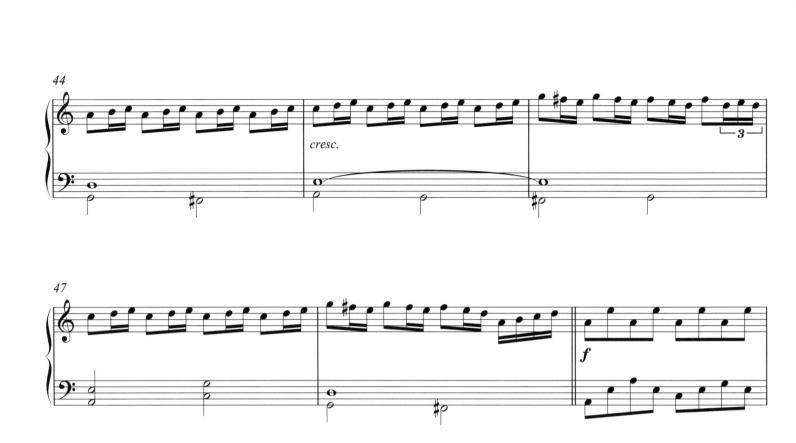

cresc.

f

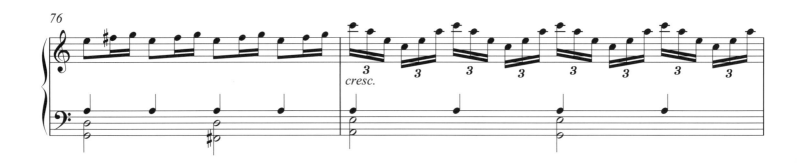

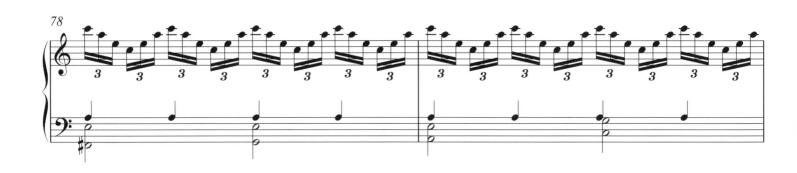

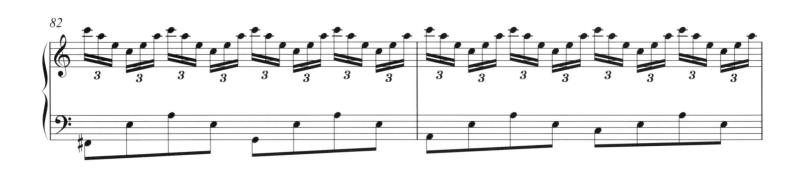

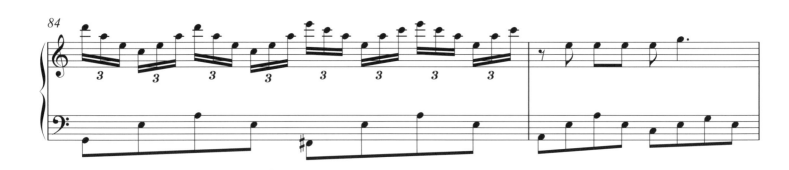

Con pedale

Walk

Music by Ludovico Einaudi

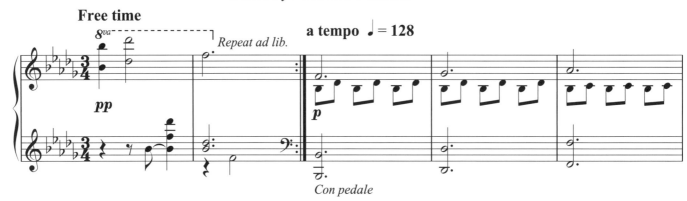

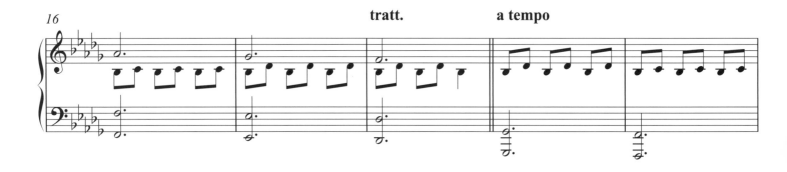

Discovery At Night

Music by Ludovico Einaudi

Andante ♩ = 60

Run

Music by Ludovico Einaudi

Free time

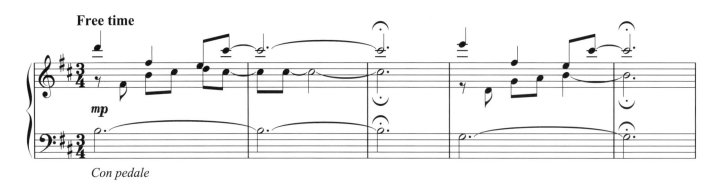

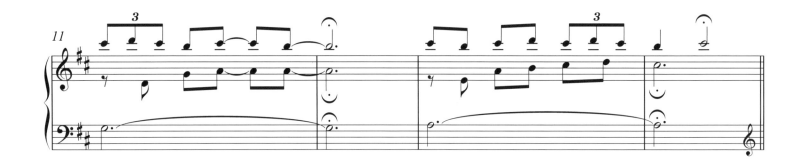

28

Brothers

Music by Ludovico Einaudi

Orbits

Music by Ludovico Einaudi

Con pedale

Two Trees

Music by Ludovico Einaudi

allarg.   a tempo   allarg.

a tempo

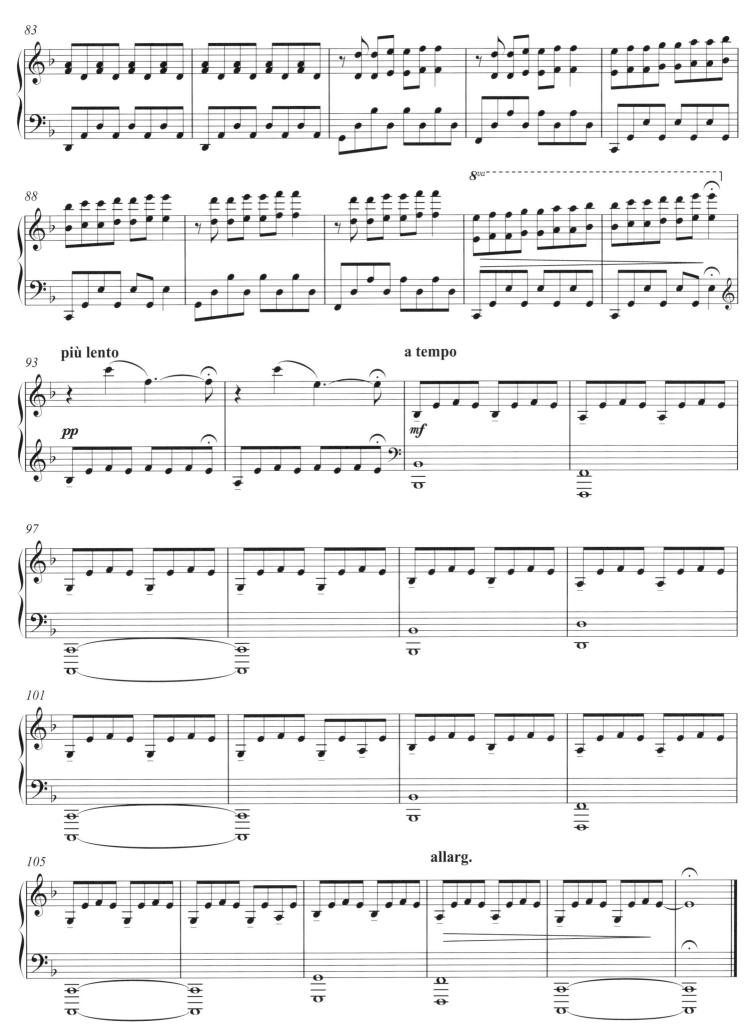

Newton's Cradle

Music by Ludovico Einaudi

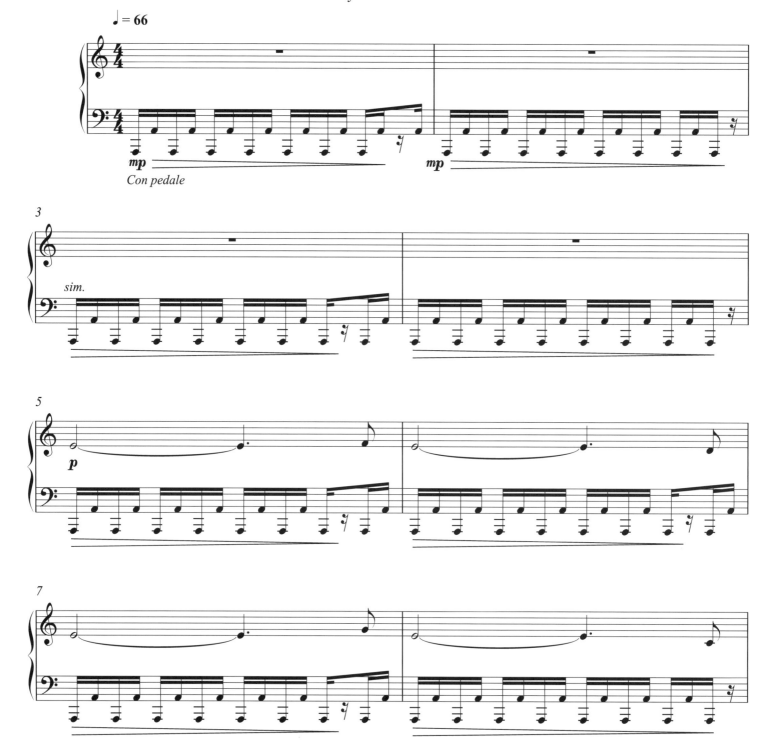

46

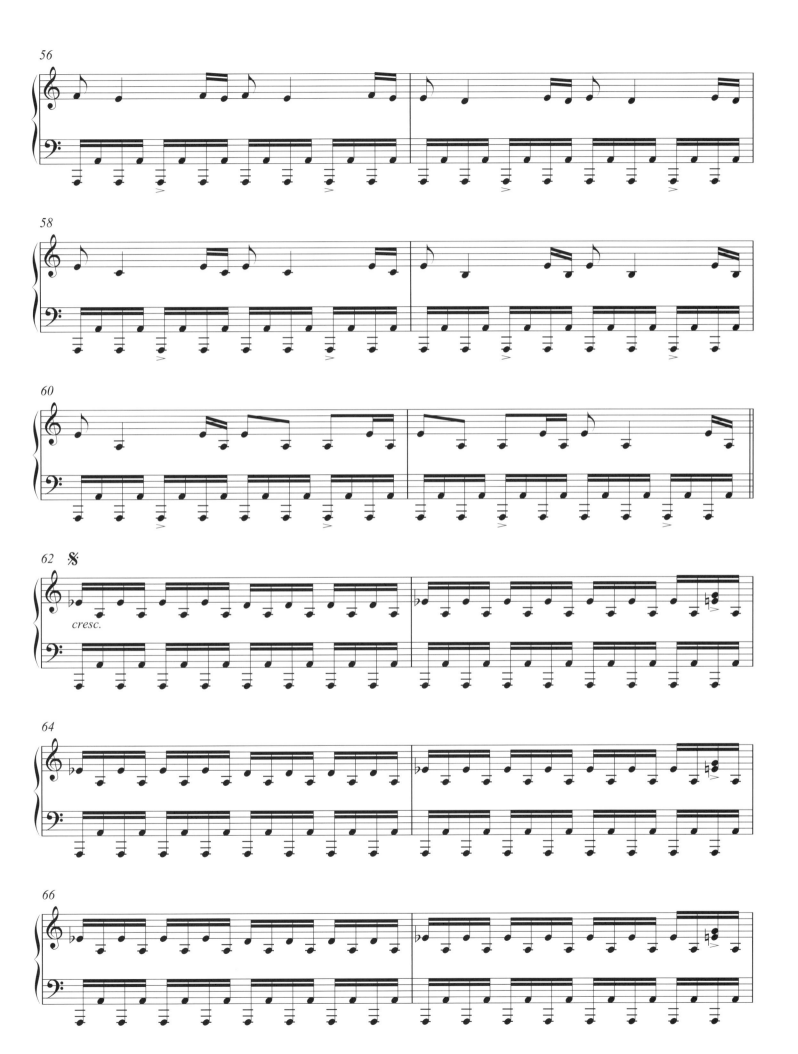

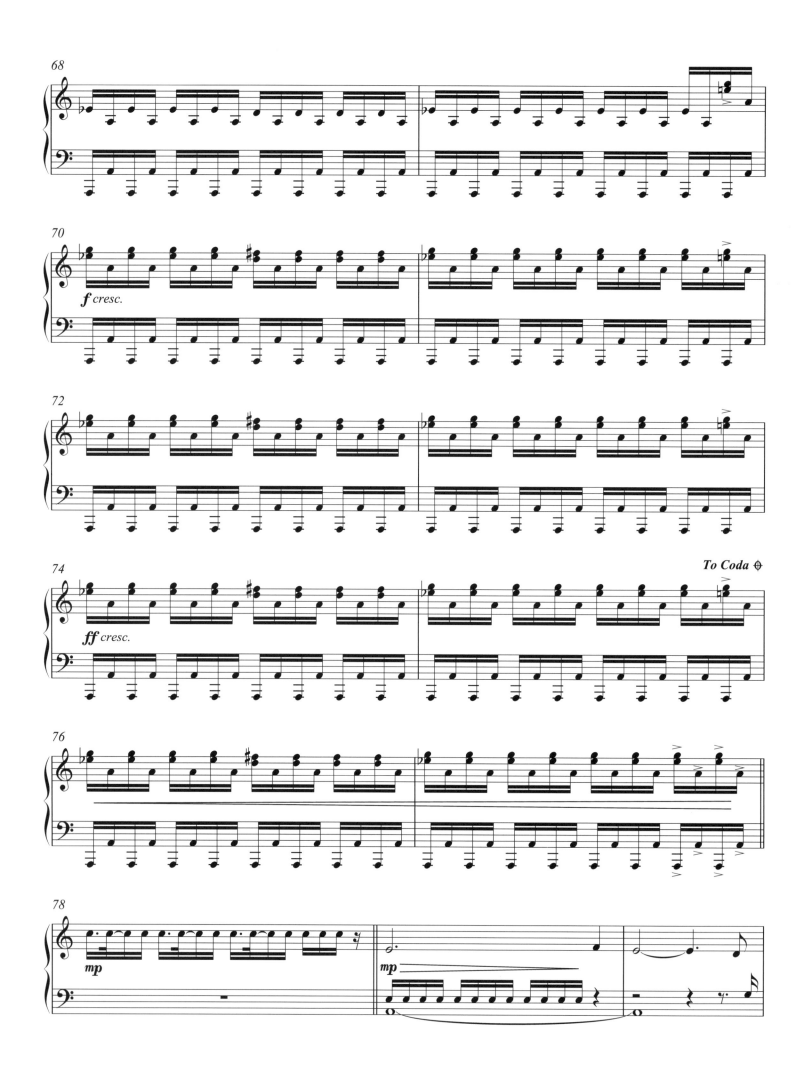

To Coda ⊕

Waterways

Music by Ludovico Einaudi

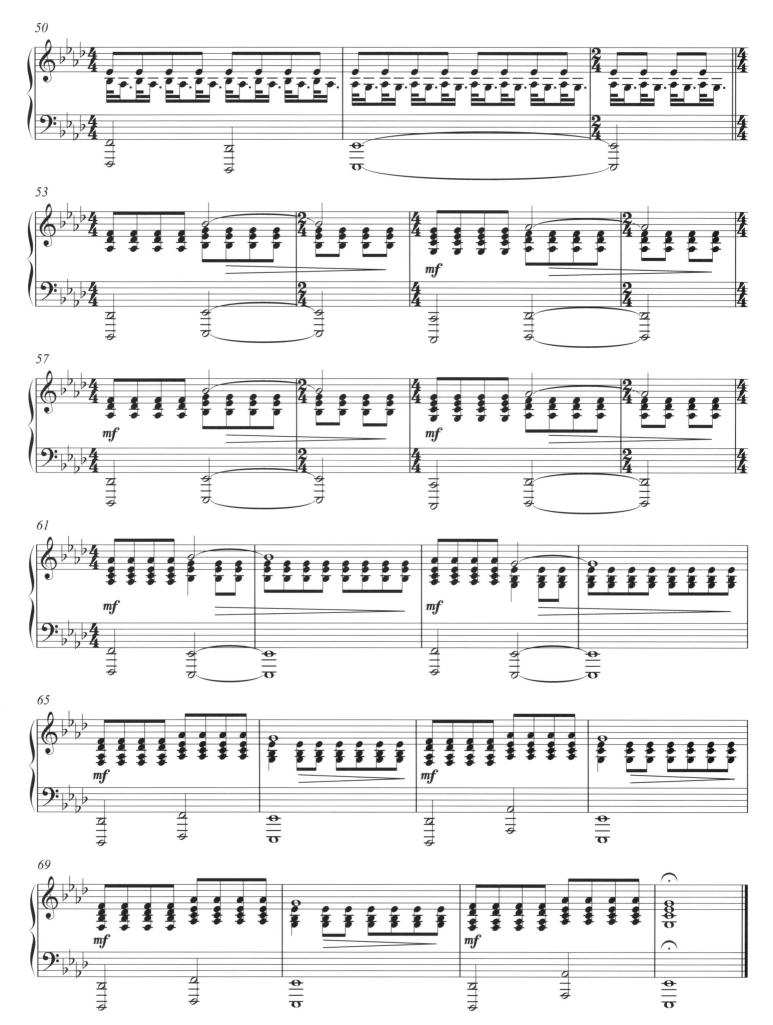

Experience

Music by Ludovico Einaudi

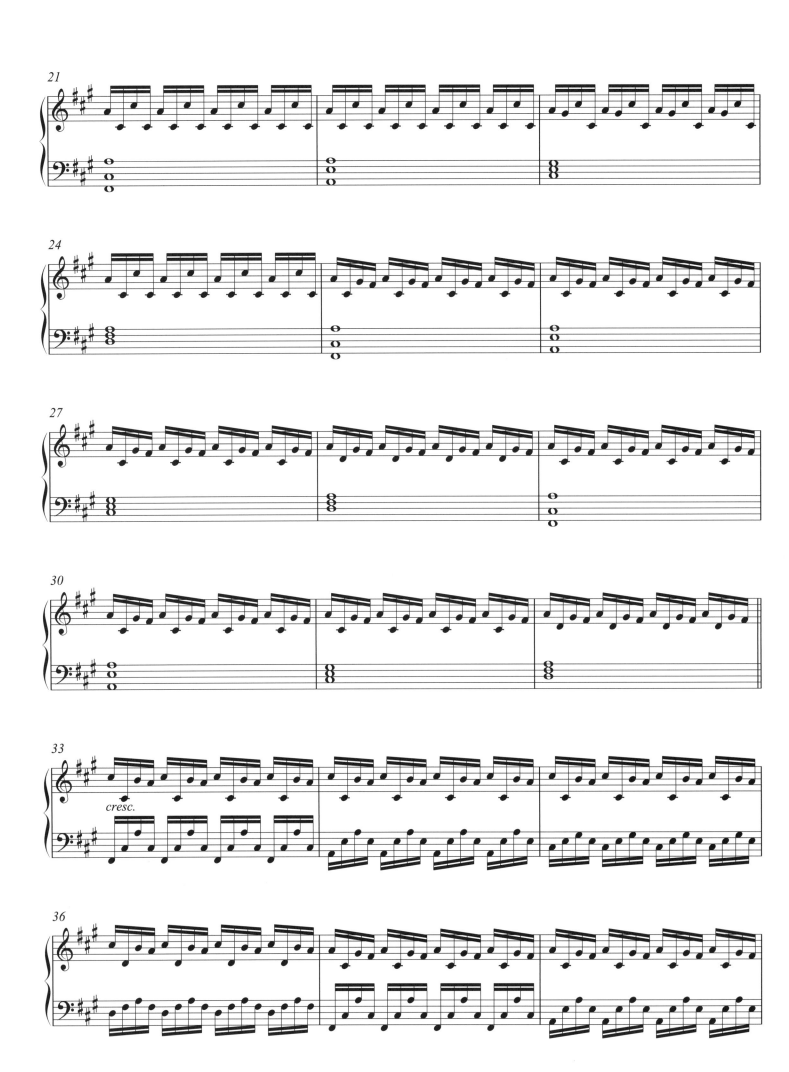

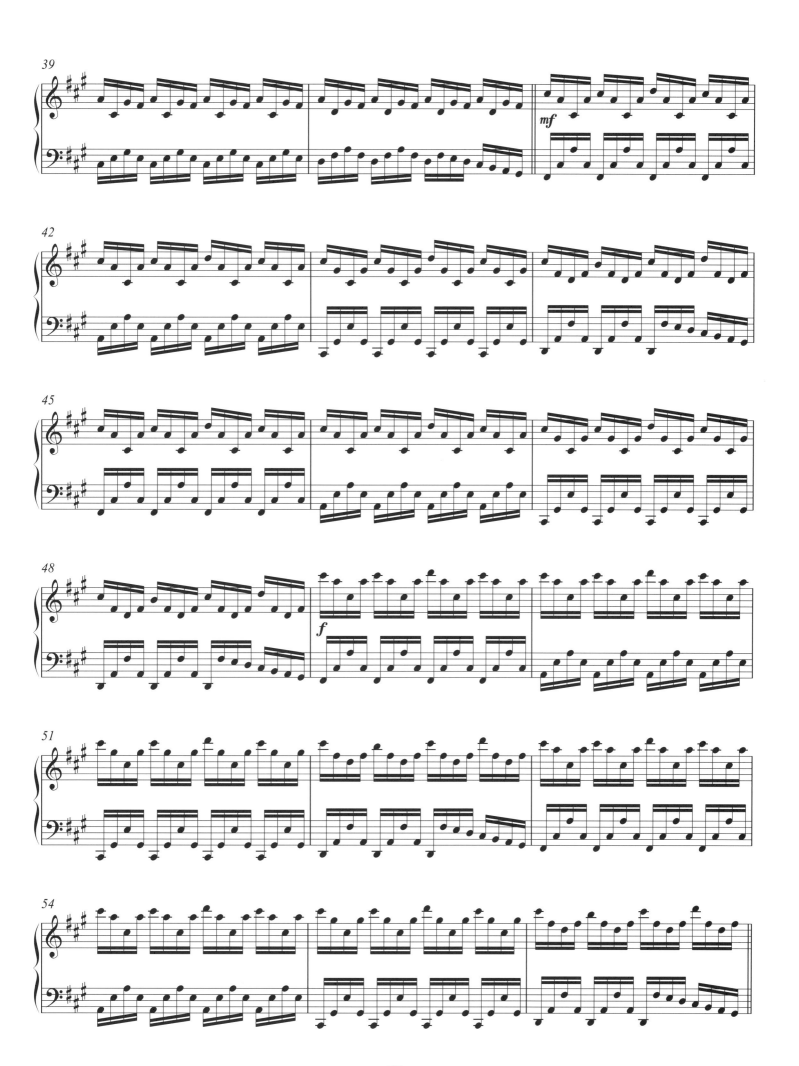

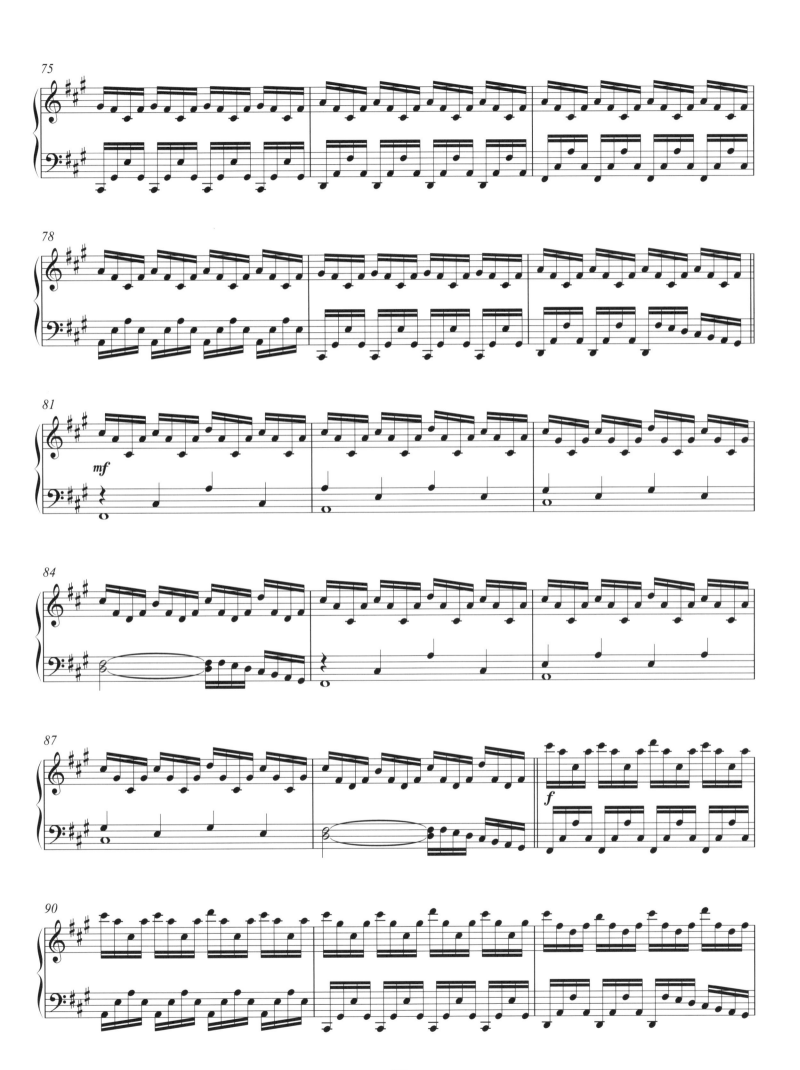

Underwood

Music by Ludovico Einaudi

Andante ♩ = 92

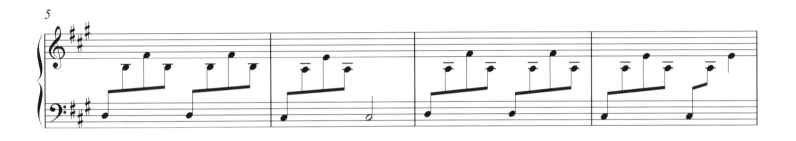

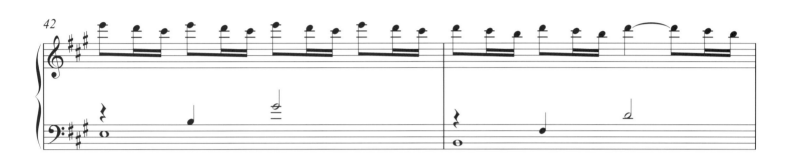

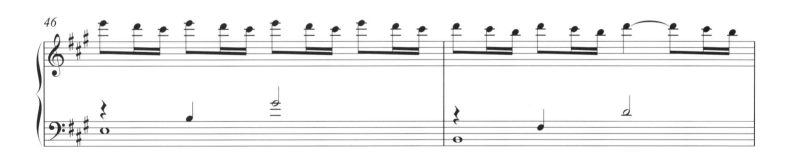

più incerto

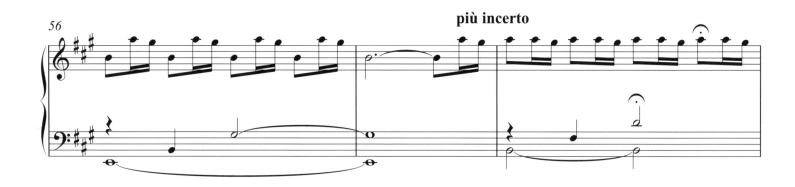

rall.

Burning

Music by Ludovico Einaudi

Bever

Music by Ludovico Einaudi

The Dark Bank Of Clouds

Music by Ludovico Einaudi

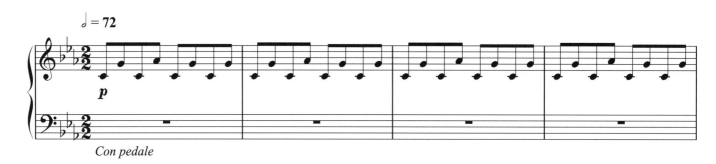

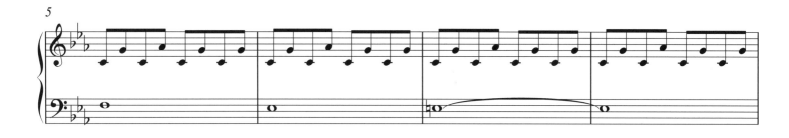

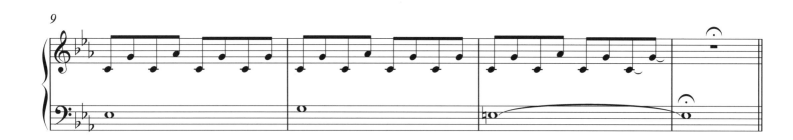

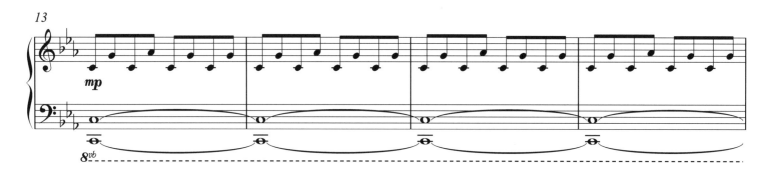

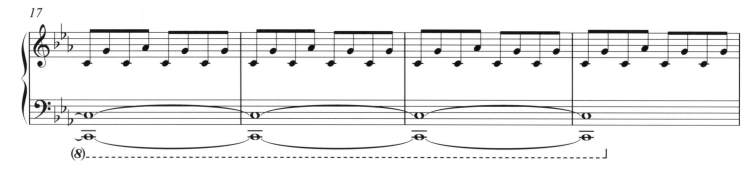

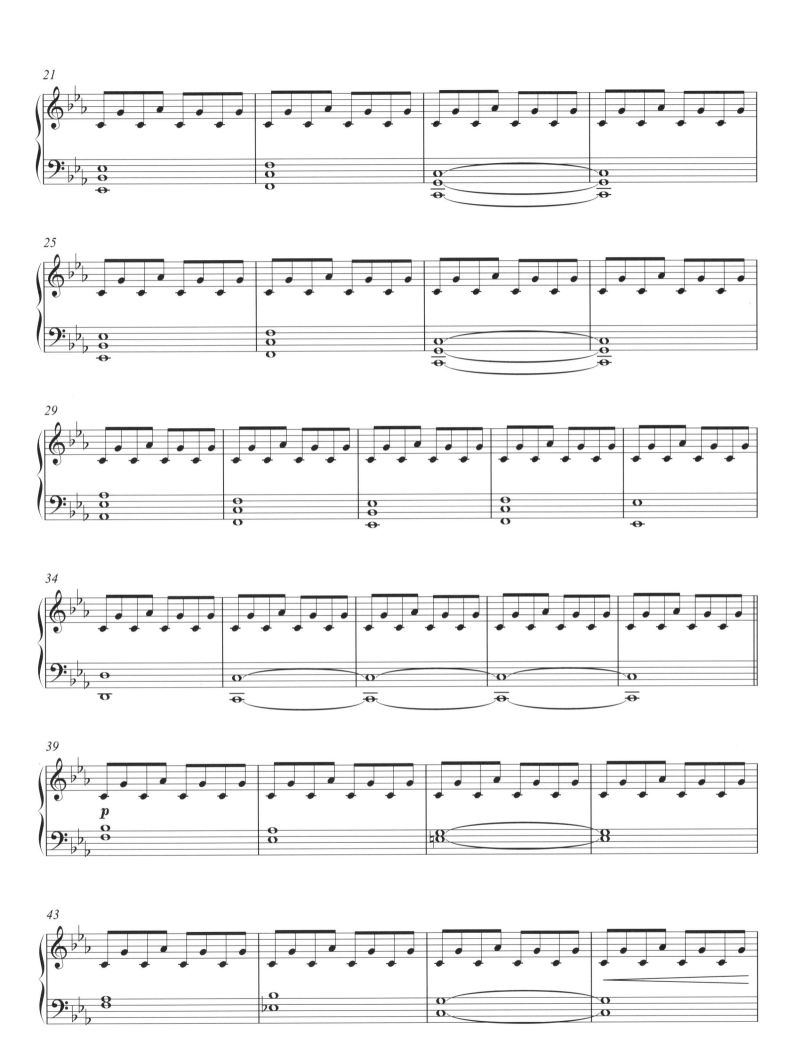

73

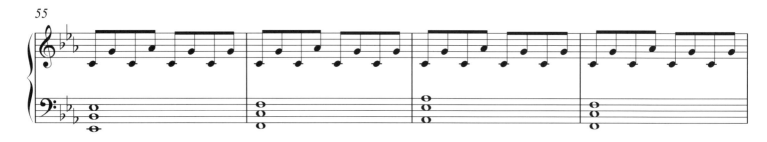

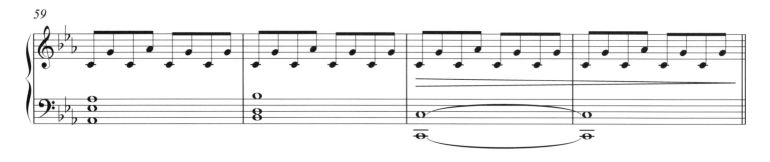

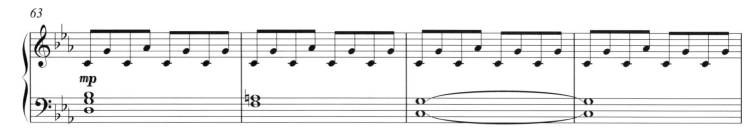

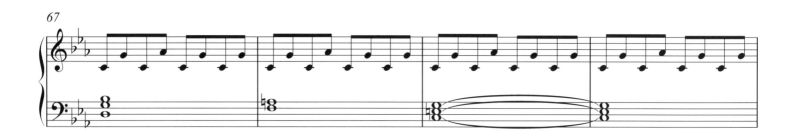

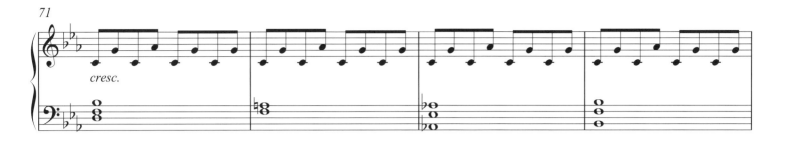

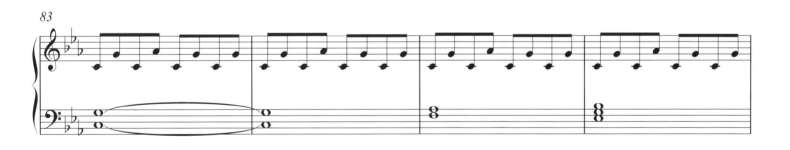

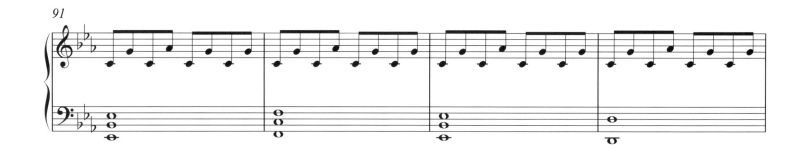

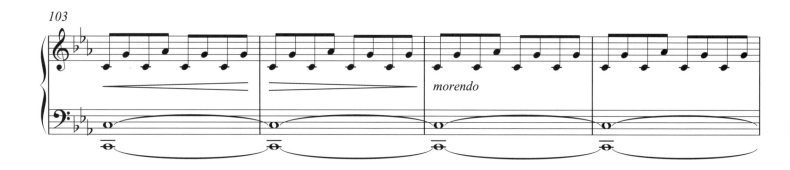

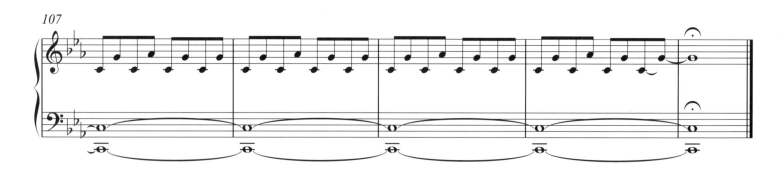

Sarabande

Music by Ludovico Einaudi

Ronald's Dream

Music by Ludovico Einaudi

Con pedale

Corale Solo

Music by Ludovico Einaudi

allarg.

Una Mattina
AM91301

Divenire
CH72006

Nightbook
CH76043

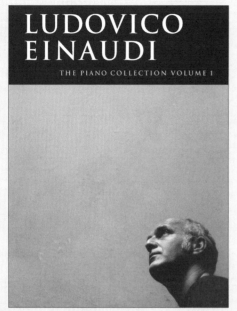
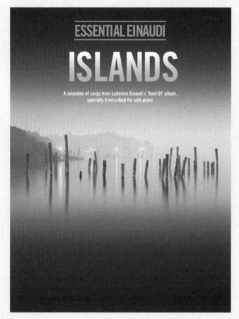
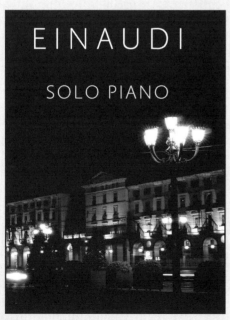